Homes

Richard Wood

Wayland

Titles in the series

Country Life

Exploration

Food

Homes

Kings and Queens

Religion

Scientists and Writers

Town Life

Cover illustrations: *Background* Rooms of a Tudor home. *Inset* A Stuart home in Cambridgeshire.

First published in 1994 by Wayland (Publishers) Ltd
61 Western Road, Hove, East Sussex BN3 1JD

Series editor: Cath Senker
Book editor: Alison Field
Designer: John Christopher
Picture researcher: Elizabeth Moore

British Library Cataloguing in Publication Data
Wood, Richard
Homes. – (Tudors and Stuarts series)
I. Title II. Series
643.0941

ISBN 0-7502-1152-0

Typeset by Strong Silent Type
Printed and bound by B.P.C.C. Paulton Books, Great Britain

Picture acknowledgements
Ancient Art & Architecture Collection 4 (below), 7 (below),10 (below), 14 (below), 15 (below); Fotomas Index *cover* (background), 13 (below), GGS Photo Graphics 12 (both), 19 (above); Ipswich Borough Council Museums 24; Manchester City Art Galleries 25 (below); Mary Rose Trust 18 (above); National Portrait Gallery 23 (above); National Trust Photographic Library 5 (below) (Bethell), 5 (above) (Williams), 11 (below) (Bloemendal), 15 (above), *cover* (foreground), *title page* & 26 (Hurst), 27 (above); Scottish National Portrait Gallery 20; Weald and Downland Open Air Museum 8 (below), 9 (both; below by Richard Harris); Weidenfeld & Nicolson 14 (above); National Museum of Wales (Welsh Folk Museum) 6, 25 (above); David Williams Picture Library 4 (above); Richard Wood 7 (above), 8 (above), 10 (above), 11 (above), 16, 17 (both), 18, 19 (below), 21 (both), 22, 23 (below).

Notes for teachers

Homes draws on a wide range of exciting sources including buildings, inventories, artefacts, paintings and drawings. This book:

◆ looks at how buildings were constructed;

◆ explains how rich and poor people lived and looks at their daily habits;

◆ describes how their homes were built, and what they contained;

◆ shows how homes developed from cold, smoky and sparsely furnished houses to more comfortable homes with glazed windows, chimneys and comfortable furniture;

◆ helps the reader to understand how we use clues from the past to learn about how people used to live then.

Contents

Tudor castles and mansions

In 1485, the Wars of the Roses ended and Henry Tudor became the first Tudor king, Henry VII.

Many rich families still lived in very strong homes. They were built like castles to protect them from attack. But in peaceful Tudor England, people soon saw that this was unnecessary.

(Above) Crathes Castle in Scotland.

At first, many great houses were still built with towers and battlements, like castles. But they would have been hard to defend against attacks. Look at the picture of Compton Wynyates to find out why.

Compton Wynyates in Warwickshire was built in 1525 using bricks, which were expensive then.

Hardwick Hall, Derbyshire, which was built in 1591–7.

The long gallery at Hardwick Hall.

In Scotland, life was often less peaceful than in England. Rich Scottish families still built castles to protect themselves from raids. How many differences can you spot between the Scottish and English homes on these two pages?

In England, some families became very rich, especially in Queen Elizabeth's reign. They wanted to show off their wealth by building huge mansions in the country.

Glass was still an expensive luxury. But grand houses such as Hardwick Hall had huge windows. People said they had 'more glass than wall'.

Upstairs, many Tudor mansions had a 'long gallery'. The walls were lined with tapestries, or with paintings of the owner's family and friends. Tall windows that looked over the gardens meant that the gallery was brightly lit.

At Hardwick, the long gallery ran the full length of the house. On dull, wet days, the family could walk here for exercise, or even play bowls. At night this was where they played music and danced.

Smaller Tudor homes

Only the richest Tudor families could afford big houses built of brick or stone. In poorer parts of Britain, quite important people often lived in strong but small houses. Y Garreg Fawr was built in 1544 for a wealthy farmer in North Wales. How many rooms do you think it had?

Most Tudor homes were even smaller than Y Garreg Fawr. They had walls of wood and mud, and roofs thatched with reed or straw. Think about where the materials came from and why most people used them.

The houses were often well built, and many are still lived in today. You can see whole streets of Tudor houses in towns such as York, Chester and Lavenham.

Y Garreg Fawr. Why do you think the Welsh farmer chose to build in stone?

A street in Lavenham, Suffolk. The town was an important centre for the wool trade.

Most homes had just one room, called the hall. This was where the people cooked, ate their food and slept. Other smaller rooms were used as stores, workshops and shops. Sometimes there was a parlour where the owner and his family sat, ate or slept.

Many poor Tudor families lived in tiny cottages with just one room. These houses were not built to last, and there are few left today. Other poor people lived as servants or workers in the homes of wealthy farmers or tradesmen.

A Tudor beggar.

Those who had no work often became homeless. They wandered from village to village, looking for jobs and begging for food.

A Tudor farmhouse

(Above) Bayleaf Farmhouse in Sussex.

Many Tudor yeomen and their families lived in homes like Bayleaf Farmhouse, which was built in the 1400s. Yeomen were people such as craftsmen, traders and farmers who owned or rented a small piece of land. Their homes had several rooms with some good furniture.

8

The upper chamber of Bayleaf Farmhouse looks as it did in Henry VIII's reign.

From outside, Bayleaf Farmhouse seems to be built in three parts. The hall is in the middle. This is a tall room with no upstairs. The timbers on the inside of the roof are black with soot from the fire burning in the middle of the floor. There is no chimney, but smoke escapes through openings in the roof. Some goes out through the windows, which have no glass.

The hall was the main living room in a Tudor farmhouse. This was where the family ate their meals and entertained friends. Food was usually cooked here. In towns, though, many people had separate kitchens to reduce the risk of fire.

(Left) Inside the hall at Bayleaf Farmhouse.

At night, servants and visitors slept in the hall, resting their straw mattresses on tables, or on the floor near the fire.

Can you see why the two ends of the farmhouse look different from the middle? They have two storeys, with stairs leading to upstairs rooms. The 'lower' end on the right contains service rooms, where goods were stored and food was prepared. The 'upper' (left) end has a best parlour with a chamber above. These more comfortable rooms were used mainly by the owner and his family.

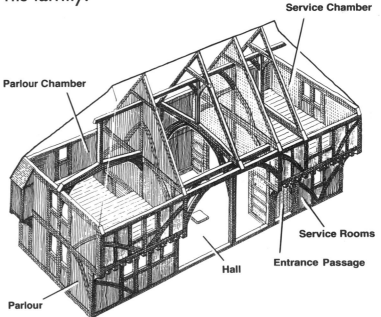

A cutaway plan of Bayleaf Farmhouse.

Parlour Chamber

Service Chamber

Service Rooms

Entrance Passage

Hall

Parlour

Building the home

The builders of most Tudor and Stuart homes used long, straight timbers from specially-grown oak trees. Other trees were also used, but were less strong.

As soon as the trees were felled, they were cut to shape. Wood is much easier to cut while it is still moist and green. Pit saws, like the one on the right, were operated by two men. It was tiring work!

A builder's pit saw. One man sawed from the top and another from below.

Many pieces of wood were joined together to make a house frame. Instead of using nails or screws, the joiners cut joints in the wood.

To hold each joint firmly in place, a hole was drilled through both pieces and a wooden peg was knocked in. Houses had many similar timbers, so builders marked them with numbers to remind them which piece went where.

A Tudor builder shapes timbers with an axe. The joints he has cut are by his feet.

The builders then carted all the pieces of wood to the house site. They pegged the walls together on the ground and hauled them into place with ropes. In the picture (left), some children in Tudor dress are helping to 'frame up' a house. Why do you think the bottom timbers rest on a low brick wall?

Once the frame was in place, the builders filled in the walls by jamming thin sticks called wattles into the gaps. Then they covered them with thick daub. This was a mixture of mud, clay, cow dung and chopped straw. When the daub dried, it set hard.

(Above) Putting up a building in the Tudor style at Kentwell Hall, Suffolk.

Paycocke's House in Essex, built in 1500. What did the builder use instead of daub to fill the gaps in the wooden frame?

1485
Henry VII brings peace after the Wars of the Roses.

1509
Thatched roofs are banned in Norwich after fire destroys the city centre.

1525
Compton Wynyates is built with mock battlements.

1534
Glass is expensive at four pennies per sheet.

1536–9
Henry VIII closes the monasteries and sells off their buildings.

Goods and chattels

In early Tudor times, most people owned very few things. Early Tudor furniture was usually very plain and simple. People sat on stools or benches. For tables they used scrubbed boards propped on trestles. They kept clothes in chests, and pegged shelves into the walls for kitchen equipment, plates, knives and spoons.

(Above) A press cupboard (a hall cupboard with shelves inside) from Queen Elizabeth's reign.

How many differences can you spot between the two cupboards on this page? The aumbrey was made by a carpenter in about 1490. He used thick oak planks held together with nails and iron bands. It is very heavy. In places the nails have split the wood. The press cupboard was made by a joiner in about 1600. Its thin, light oak panels are set in a strong frame. The frame is held in place by joints and pegs, like a timber-framed house.

An aumbrey, a cupboard that can be locked.

12

When people died, their friends wrote lists of their goods and chattels. These inventories give us useful information about Tudor and Stuart homes.

Thomas Roger was a Norfolk fisherman who died in 1587. His cottage probably had only two rooms. He kept his clothes in 'two littell cofferes' (chests). He also had an 'oulde aumbrye', probably like the one in the photograph on page 12.

Wooden and pewter tableware used on Henry VIII's ship *Mary Rose*, which sank in 1545.

An early Tudor kitchen in a poor farmer's house. The things on the table are made from pewter.

Thomas kept 'eight pound of puter' (pewter) objects in his aumbrey. He had no chairs, but he did have three stools and two table-tops. He also had a bed and some kitchen equipment, but that was about all!

By Stuart times, even poor people had several pieces of furniture. The rich could now buy a lot of different furnishings. Curtains, table carpets and soft cushions brought luxury to their homes.

Home work

Many Tudor and Stuart people worked at home. Some men and women went out every day to work on the land. But most people hardly ever (or never) left the villages where they were born. Only rich lords, landowners or merchants had the chance to travel much.

Inventories, like Thomas Roger's, often give us clues about the work people did. We know that Thomas was a fisherman, because he kept nets, ropes, 'an oulde botte' (old boat) and fish at home.

The kitchen of a big Stuart House.

His inventory also lists 'one spinninge whele'. Until powerful machines for spinning and weaving were invented in the 1700s, these jobs were done by hand. It was slow work, usually done at home by women and children. Merchants travelled from cottage to cottage collecting the finished products. Even rich women spent many hours every day doing needlework.

Tudor spinsters and weavers. What does 'spinster' mean today?

Women usually had to cook as well. See how many different jobs are being done in the large Stuart kitchen on the left. Look at all the equipment.

Thomas Roger had only 'one brasse potte, one kettill and two littell pannes' to cook with. He also had a spit for roasting meat, as in the picture.

(Above) This Stuart tapestry shows the 'pleasure garden' of a rich home.

Most homes had gardens where the housewife grew vegetables and herbs. Tudor gardens were often divided into square beds, each for a different type of plant. Some were 'pot herbs' for flavouring food. Others were used for medicines. Popular flowers were gillyflowers (carnations) and marigolds. Even these were used in cooking.

A Tudor lady waters a rosemary bush.

15

Elizabethan improvements

In 1577, William Harrison wrote a 'Description of England'. He said that old men in his Somerset village found 'three things to be marvellously altered' since they were children. They slept in better beds. They ate off pewter plates instead of wooden ones. And a number of chimneys had recently been built. For many people, life was becoming more comfortable.

Most early Tudor homes were very smoky from the fires burning in the middle of the floor. But during the reigns of Elizabeth I and James I, chimneys became much more common. Cheaper bricks meant that even quite poor people could afford them. People built new homes with chimneys or added them to older houses.

Houses with chimneys were warmer, less draughty and less smelly. Fabrics such as clothes and bed linen did not always smell of smoke. Furniture and decorations were not blackened by soot. With fires now burning safely out of the way, there was no need for such high rooms. People could build upper floors over their old open halls and make their living space bigger with new chambers.

Pendean Farmhouse, Sussex, was built in Queen Elizabeth's reign. Why do you think the chimney was so big?

Wealthy Elizabethans often had wide staircases built next to the chimney. They led to all the upper rooms. By 1600, window glass was also becoming more common.

(Left) Stuart windows were glazed with many small panes of glass, held in place with strips of lead.

Timeline

1560–1640
The Great Rebuilding of England. Many homes are rebuilt or enlarged.

1590
Glass now costs two pennies per sheet. Hardwick Hall is built.

1596
Harrington invents the first flush toilet.

The photograph (right) of a house in Lavenham shows another common improvement. Extra rooms were built out from the back of the house. Often these were service rooms, such as kitchens, dairies or wash rooms. The work areas were now separate from the living rooms of the house.

The Priory at Lavenham, Suffolk. How many extensions can you see?

Conveniences

Today, we depend on services such as electricity, gas, water and drains. Have you ever had a power cut or a blocked drain at home? Perhaps it reminded you that life was not always so easy.

In Tudor and Stuart times, most people burnt wood for warmth and for cooking. In Tudor fireplaces, logs often rested on fire dogs. These were iron bars, shaped like dogs with long necks. They stopped long logs from rolling onto the floor.

Not many people burnt coal in Tudor times. By late Stuart times, though, deeper coal mines had been dug, and coal became more common. Coal did not burn well in wide old Tudor fireplaces. People bricked parts of them up, and fitted narrow iron grates instead.

Logs burning in a Tudor fireplace. The metal bars around it are called fire dogs.

After dark, candles were lit. These were usually made from smelly tallow (animal fat) saved from the drippings of roasting meat. Rushes could be dipped in fat to make rushlights, which were cheaper than candles.

(Right) An upstairs toilet at Bayleaf Farmhouse. Where do you think it emptied?

(Below) Candles, rushlights and holders.

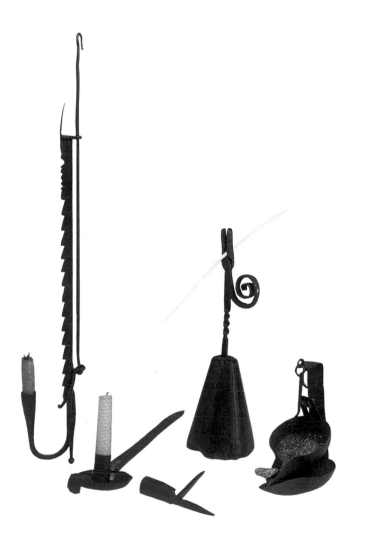

Tudor toilets were often smelly, too. Most people used a cesspit, a hole in the ground outdoors, with a seat over it. Chamber-pots were kept indoors and emptied into the pit after use. Lazy people sometimes tipped the contents out of their windows into street drains.

In 1596, John Harrison invented the first water-closet, flushed by water from a lake. Queen Elizabeth saw it and had one built at Richmond Palace, but the idea was soon forgotten.

Instead of toilet paper, people used plant leaves or pieces of cloth. Today, archaeologists sometimes find them preserved in old cesspits.

Children at home

Most Tudor and Stuart families had two or three children. Even in rich families, many babies were born dead. One in five children died before their first birthday, and four in ten died before their teens. Very few people lived long enough to be grandparents.

Boys could marry at fourteen, girls at twelve or sometimes even younger. But this was not common, and poor people did not usually marry until their mid-twenties. They preferred to wait until they could afford a decent home.

In rich homes, nurses were paid to look after small children. When they were about seven, rich boys sometimes went away to school. Girls stayed at home, and were taught by tutors or their mothers.

The Countess of Rothes and her daughters at home in 1626.

(Above) Writing with a pen made from a goose feather is harder than it looks!

The Babees Book told children how to behave at home:

"*When entering a room ... say 'God speed', and with humble cheer greet all who are present.*"

Children were not to hack their meat, scratch their hair or wipe their noses on the tablecloth!

Poor children did not usually go to school. Boys went to work in the fields from the age of four or five. Girls worked at home, spinning wool, cooking or growing food. Life for them was very hard.

Many rich Tudor children went away to work as pages or servants for other families. Middle-class boys became apprentices to merchants or craftsmen. This surprised an Italian visitor:

"*Everyone sends away his children into the houses of others, whilst he, in return, receives those of strangers into his own.*"

Children in Tudor costume working in the fields at Kentwell Hall, Suffolk. What are they doing?

Comfort and colour

By 1600, many homes had chimneys and glazed windows. Smoke and cold were less of a problem than before. More wealthy people could make their homes attractive and comfortable to live in.

Parlours were often brightly decorated. Wallpaper had been made in London since 1520, but it was very expensive. Instead, many people painted the timbers of their rooms. Red was a popular colour. Sometimes walls were covered with a thin coat of plaster. Painters travelled from house to house, decorating walls with bold patterns and figures known as 'antique work'.

The parlour of the house below in Debenham once had the same big pattern repeated six times round its walls. The red initials in the centre of the pattern remind us who lived there in the 1580s – a butcher and his wife called William and Mary Mottes.

An Elizabethan wall painting in Debenham, Suffolk.

For seats, most people still had only hard stools and benches. But inventories of better-off Tudors suggest that they sometimes padded the stools with soft cushions.

Important people, such as the men at Somerset House (right), sat on chairs with backs and arms. Today, we still call the head of a company or meeting the 'chair' or 'chairperson'. Look at the carpet spread over the table. Until the end of Stuart times, carpets were not put on the floor. They were used as table coverings.

The Somerset House Conference, 1604. What tells you that these are important people?

From the 1660s, furniture with soft coverings became common in the homes of rich people. Perhaps people had begun to notice how uncomfortable their seats were.

The daybed was a fashionable item, particularly for women. They could stretch out on it as we might on a sofa today.

A Stuart daybed from about 1680.

And so to bed ...

In Tudor and Stuart times, the word 'bed' meant mattress. What we call a bed was known as a bedstead. Poor people often had no bedsteads. They slept on straw beds on the floor. Others had 'box beds' built into the wall, like big cupboards.

The best bedsteads had posts at each corner, supporting a roof called a 'tester'. At night people drew curtains right round the bed to keep themselves warm and private. Rooms usually led off each other, so people often had to walk past beds where others were sleeping. Until late Stuart times, there were no separate, private bedrooms. People slept in halls and parlours as well as in upstairs rooms.

The bed on the left shows the sort of beautiful bed hangings owned by rich people. The women of the house were often skilled needleworkers. They loved to embroider their hangings with colourful flowers, birds and insects.

The object on the bed is a 'bed waggon'. It held smouldering logs or coals to warm and air the sheets.

The Stuart bedchamber at Christchurch Mansion, Ipswich.

The small Welsh bedstead (left) is a 'trundle' or 'truckle' bed. During the day it was stored under the main bed. At night it was 'trundled' out, perhaps for children or servants to sleep on. (Did you spot another one earlier in this book?)

A seventeenth-century Welsh truckle bed. What makes it move easily?

Lady Aston (right) is propped up in bed. Rich people used many layers of feather beds and pillows. They liked to sleep on a slope with their heads higher than their feet. Poles, called 'bed staffs', were stuck into the sides of the bed to stop the sleeping person from rolling out.

Sir Thomas Aston's bedroom, 1636. Can you work out the story this picture tells?

1621
A new way of making glass is invented. Price falls to one penny per sheet.

About 1650
Many village brickworks start up. Bricks become cheaper.

About 1660
Furniture becomes softer. The chest of drawers is invented.

1666
The Great Fire of London destroys many homes. The city is rebuilt in brick and stone.

1702–14
Reign of Queen Anne, the last Stuart. There is a fashion for square brick houses.

The end of an age

Many late Stuart houses were quite different from Tudor homes. From outside, they had a square, balanced look. Inside, each room had a special use. For many people, home life was more convenient than ever before.

Most poor people still lived in tiny, timber-framed cottages. But even they now had chimneys and glazed windows. Better-off people usually plastered their walls outside and inside to hide the timber frame. The plaster also helped to keep the warmth in. Sometimes it was moulded into patterns or painted in bright colours.

A Stuart gentleman's home in Wisbech, Cambridgeshire. Notice how neat and square it looks.

In Wales, farmers often painted their homes red. They thought this would protect them against evil spirits.

Many people hid old clothes or shoes or dead cats up chimneys to stop bad spirits entering at night.

(Above) **This room at Packwood House, Warwickshire, contains tapestries and furniture from 1680–1700.**

After about 1660, most big homes were square-shaped and built of stone or bricks. They had a central front door, with a hall and stairs behind. All the rooms led off the hall and landing. This convenient layout also made each room private from the others.

Wealthy people could now buy many new types of furniture. Chests of drawers gradually replaced chests for keeping clothes in. Chair seats were often woven from split cane, or padded with soft fabric. Mirror frames, cupboards and writing desks were made of light walnut wood instead of oak.

The best furniture was decorated with thin strips of coloured woods to make patterns. You can see some of these new styles in the picture above of the gallery at Packwood House.

Timeline

| 1480 | 1500 | 1520 | 1540 | 1560 | 1580 |

Tudors

1485 HENRY VII
1509 HENRY VIII
1547 EDWARD VI
1553 MARY TUDOR
1558 ELIZABETH I

1480–1500	1500–1520	1520–1540	1540–1560	1560–1580	1580–1600
1485 Battle of Bosworth ends the Wars of the Roses.	**1500–1547** Sheep farmers enclose common land.	**1520** The Spanish start to colonize the American mainland.	**1543** Andreas Vesalius publishes his book about the human body.	**1560s** Francis Drake makes voyages with John and William Hawkins.	**1582** The modern calendar is introduced in Europe by Pope Gregory XIII.
1487 The Court of Star Chamber punishes people who are a danger to the king.	**1507** America is named after Amerigo Vespucci.	**1530** Thomas Cromwell gains more power on the death of Cardinal Wolsey.	**1545** The *Mary Rose* sinks.	**1567** Mary Queen of Scots flees to England but is imprisoned in England.	**1584** Tobacco and potatoes are first brought to England by Sir Walter Raleigh.
1492 Columbus sails to the West Indies.	**1509** Henry Cabot tries to sail round the north of Canada.	**1534** Henry VIII makes himself Head of the Church in England.	**1547–1553** Many new schools and colleges are founded.	**1577** Francis Drake sets off on his voyage around the world.	**1587** Mary Queen of Scots is executed.
1497 John Cabot discovers Newfoundland.	**1515** Cardinal Wolsey becomes Lord Chancellor.	**1535** First printed English Bible. Sir Thomas More, the Lord Chancellor, is executed.	**1549** Robert Kett leads a rebellion in Norfolk.		**1588** The Spanish Armada is defeated by the English fleet.
	1517 Martin Luther starts the Reformation in Germany.	**1536–39** Henry VIII has the monasteries destroyed.	**1553–58** Protestants are persecuted and put to death under Queen Mary.		**1590–1616** William Shakespeare writes his plays.

1600 1620 1640 1660 1680 1700

Stuarts

1603 JAMES I (JAMES VI OF SCOTLAND)

1625 CHARLES I

1649–1660 COMMONWEALTH
1653 OLIVER CROMWELL

1658 RICHARD CROMWELL

1660 CHARLES II

1685 JAMES II

1688 WILLIAM III & MARY II

1702–1714 ANNE

1600–1620

1601
The Poor Law provides help for poor people.

1603
The English and Scottish crowns are united in the Stuart King James.

1605
The Gunpowder Plot.

1607
Henry Hudson sets off to explore the coast of Canada

1610
Tea is first drunk in Europe and soon arrives in Britain.

1620–1640

1620
The Pilgrim Fathers sail to America.

1623
The composer William Byrd dies.

1628
William Harvey describes how blood goes round the body.

1629–1640
Charles I rules without Parliament.

1640
The Scots defeat Charles I.

1640–1660

1642
The English Civil War begins.

1646
Charles I is captured and imprisoned.

1649
Charles I is executed.

1650
The first coffee house opens, in Oxford.

1653–1658
Oliver Cromwell rules as Lord Protector.

1660–1680

1660
Charles II restores the monarchy.

1665
The Great Plague.

1666
The Great Fire of London.

1660–1669
Samuel Pepys writes his diary.

1660–1685
Hooke and Newton study light and gravity.
Sir Christopher Wren designs many new buildings.

1680–1700

1680–1695
Henry Purcell writes his music.

1688
The Glorious Revolution: James II flees.

1690
James II is defeated at the Battle of the Boyne.

1694
Queen Mary dies. The Bank of England is founded.

1700–1720

1707
England and Scotland are officially united.

1714
The Stuart period ends with the death of Queen Anne. George I becomes the first Hanoverian king.

Glossary

Apprentices Young people who learn a craft from a skilled master.

Archaeologists People who study the remains of the past.

Battlements Tops of walls with openings to shoot arrows or guns through.

Chamber A room, usually upstairs.

Chattel Something a person owns that can be moved from place to place.

Felled Chopped down.

Frame The skeleton of a wooden building.

Glazed Windows filled with glass.

Joiner Someone who makes joints.

Joints Pieces of wood that slot together, like plugs into sockets.

Merchant A businessman involved in trading goods.

Parlour A best sitting-room.

Pewter A grey metal made from lead and tin, often used for plates and cups.

Pit saw A long, two-handled saw for sawing big pieces of wood over a pit.

Rushes Grass-like marsh plants with thick stems.

Spinsters Tudor: people who spin wool. Modern: unmarried women.

Spit A long spike on which meat was placed for roasting.

Tallow Animal fat and dripping used for making candles.

Tapestries Wall coverings woven with pictures.

Tester A roof over a bed.

Tradesmen People who make a living buying and selling goods.

Trestles Fold-away legs for supporting a table-top.

Tutor A teacher who teaches just one person or a small group.

Wars of the Roses Wars between the Yorkist and Lancastrian families, who both claimed the right to rule England.

Books to read

Childs, A. *Under the Rose: Tudor Spy Story* (Anglia Young Books, 1991)

Howarth, S. *Renaissance Places* (Simon & Schuster, 1992)

Kelly, T. *Children in Tudor England* (Thornes and Hulton, 1987)

Lines, C. *Exploring Houses and Homes* (Wayland, 1989)

Mountfield, A. *Looking Back at Houses and Homes* (Macmillan, 1988)

Triggs, T. D. *Tudor and Stuart Times* (Folens, 1992)

Unstead, R. J. *Houses* (A & C Black, 1986)

Places to visit

England
Avon: Dyram Park, Chippenham. (0272) 372501
Cambridgeshire: Oliver Cromwell's House, Ely. (0353) 662062
Cheshire: Bramhall Hall, Stockport. (061) 485 3708
Little Moreton Hall, Congleton. (0260) 272018
Cornwall: Cotehele, Saltash. (0579) 50434
Cumbria: Levens Hall, Kendal. (05395) 60321
Derbyshire: Eyam Hall, Eyam. (0433) 631976
Hardwick Hall, Chesterfield. (0246) 850430
Devon: Buckland Abbey, Yelverton. (0822) 853607
Dorset: Athelhampton House, Puddeltown. (0305) 848492
Kingston Lacey, Wimbourne Minster. (0202) 883402
Essex: Ingatestone Hall, Chelmsford. (0277) 353010
Paycocke's, Coggeshall. (0376) 561305
Hampshire: The Vyne, Sherborne St John. (0256) 881337
Kent: Knole, Sevenoaks. (0732) 450608

Lancashire: Gawthorpe Hall, Burnley. (0282) 778511
Leicestershire: Doddington Hall, Doddington. (0522) 694308
Lincolnshire: Gainsborough Old Hall, Gainsborough. (0427) 612669
Woolsthorpe Manor, Colsterworth. (0476) 860338
London: Geffrye Museum. (071) 739 9893
Ham House, Richmond. (081) 940 1950
Museum of London. (071) 600 3699
Merseyside: Speke Hall, Liverpool. (051) 427 7231
Norfolk: Ancient House, Thetford. (0842) 752599
Blicking Hall, Aylsham. (0263) 733084
Strangers' Hall, Norwich. (0603) 667229
Northamptonshire: Canons Ashby House, Daventry. (0327) 860044
Shropshire: Benthall Hall, Brosely. (0952) 882159
Somerset: Montacute House, Montacute. (0935) 823289
Suffolk: Kentwell Hall, Long Melford. (0787) 310207
The Priory, Lavenham. (0787) 247417
Sussex: Weald and Downland Museum, Singleton. (0243) 63348
Warwickshire: Packwood House, Solihull. (0564) 782024

Shakespeare's Birthplace and Anne Hathaway's Cottage. (0789) 204016
Yorkshire: East Riddlesden Hall, Keighley. (0535) 607075

Wales
Cardiff: Welsh Folk Museum, St Fagans. (0222) 569441
Dyfed: Tudor Merchant's House, Tenby. (0834) 2279

Scotland
Aberdeen: Drum Castle. (03308) 204
Angus: Glamis Castle, Glamis. (0307) 84242
Dumfriesshire: Drumlanrig Castle, Thornhill. (0848) 31682
Edinburgh: Gladstone's Land. (031) 226 5856
Huntly House Museum. (031) 225 2424
Fife: Falkland Palace, Falkland. (0337) 311202
Kellie Castle, Arbroath. (03338) 271

Northern Ireland
Belfast: Ulster Folk Museum, Holywood. (02320) 428428
Co. Londonderry: Springhill, Moneymore. (06487) 48210

Index

Words printed in **bold** are subjects that appear in pictures as well as text.